the shape of things

NEIL LABUTE

the shape of things

faber and faber

Faber and Faber, Inc.
An affiliate of Farrar, Straus and Giroux
18 West 18th Street, New York 10011

First published in 2001
by Faber and Faber Limited
3 Queen Square, London WC1N 3AU

A CIP record for this book
is available from the British Library

ISBN-13: 978-0-571-21246-0
ISBN-10: 0-571-21246-8

www.fsgbooks.com

17   18   16

the shape of things premièred in london at the almeida
theatre on 24 may 2001 with the following cast:

evelyn rachel weisz
adam paul rudd
jenny gretchen mol
phillip frederick weller

director neil labute
set design giles cadle
costume design lynette meyer
lighting mark henderson
sound fergus o'hare
casting fiona weir
assistant director david salter

production manager james crout
company manager rupert carlile
stage manager lisa buckley
deputy stage manager lorna earl
assistant stage manager simon wilcock
head of wardrobe edward gibbon

characters

evelyn
adam
jenny
phillip

setting

a liberal arts college
in a conservative midwestern town

author's note

the / in certain lines denotes
an attempt at interruption or overlap
by a given character

A MUSEUM

silence. darkness.

a young woman stands near a stretch of velvet rope.
she has a can in one hand and stares up at an enormous
human sculpture. after a moment, a young man (in
uniform) steps across the barrier and approaches her.

                    ADAM
. . . you stepped over the line. miss? / umm, you stepped
over . . .

                    EVELYN
i know. / it's 'ms.'

                    ADAM
okay, sorry, ms., but, ahh . . .

                    EVELYN
i meant to. / step over . . .

                    ADAM
what? / yeah, i figured you did. i mean, the way you did
it and all, kinda deliberate like. / you're not supposed to
do that.

                    EVELYN
i know. / that's why i tried it . . .

                    ADAM
why?

EVELYN

. . . to see what would happen.

ADAM

oh. well . . . me, i s'pose.

EVELYN

'me?'

ADAM

no, i mean, i'm what happens, i guess. i have to walk over, like i've done, and ask you to take a step back. could you, please? / step back?

EVELYN

and if someone doesn't? / what then?

ADAM

. . . you're not gonna step back?

EVELYN

no . . . i mean, yes, i probably will, but just for interest's sake, what would you do if?

ADAM

i'm . . . geez, i'm not sure. i've never had anyone not step back. i've only said it, like, four times, and every time they've done it. stepped back.

EVELYN

what if i'm your first? non-stepper, i mean. then what?

ADAM

hell, i dunno . . . i'm off in, like, ten minutes, i'd probably just stand here, make sure you didn't touch anything.

EVELYN

really?

ADAM

pretty much, yeah. i'd let next shift talk to you, kick you
out or whatever.

EVELYN

you wouldn't grab me or anything?

ADAM

nah. that's too . . . you know. that's a total hassle, you
end up rolling around on the ground, you'd probably sue
the place, or me, and then . . . i'd get fired for doing my
job. screw that . . . (*beat.*) could you do that for me,
though?

EVELYN

which, roll around on the ground or sue you?

ADAM

no, step back behind the line there . . . i'd appreciate it.

EVELYN

not really.

ADAM

no, seriously, i would. i'd definitely appreciate it . . .

EVELYN

i mean, 'not really' i'm not going to . . .

ADAM

i thought you just said you probably will . . .

EVELYN

yeah, 'probably.' i decided not to.

ADAM

hey, you're not gonna mess up my weekend with this, are you?

EVELYN

i wasn't planning on it, but . . . i'm not completely against it, either.

ADAM

see, if you get all crazy, then i gotta write up a report and stuff, i'm here till six, six-thirty easy, and i have a second job to get to.

EVELYN

tonight? *friday* night?

ADAM

yep. right after this, at the video store . . .

EVELYN

why would anyone work two jobs on friday night?

ADAM

. . . for money.

EVELYN

of course . . . sorry. (*looks at him again.*) oh . . . oh, right! that's where i . . . i've seen you in there. you helped me once, i think.

ADAM

yeah? / with what?

4

EVELYN

uh-huh. / *the picture of dorian gray* . . . you found it in
classics, not drama. / somebody'd misplaced it . . .

ADAM

right, i remember that. / yes . . . behind *cabaret*. the 'joel
grey' fiasco . . .

EVELYN

yeah, you said you found it with *dirty dancing* once, too,
or something . . .

ADAM

i did, you're right . . . that's funny.

EVELYN

anyway, you helped me, that was nice . . .

ADAM

thanks. but, you're not gonna return the favour, right?

EVELYN

you mean the . . .?

  she points back toward the velvet rope.

ADAM

yeah.

EVELYN

no, sorry, i can't.

ADAM

why is that? (*pointing*) it's a pretty good-sized sculpture.
you can see it just fine from there . . .

EVELYN

truthfully? i'm building up my nerve, and if i go back
over, i'll probably be a big wuss about it and take off . . .

ADAM

about what? the 'wuss' part, i mean . . .

EVELYN

i was going to deface the statue.

ADAM

oh. oh . . . (*pointing*) is that paint?

EVELYN

yes.

ADAM

great . . . from across the room, i thought you were
maybe one of the cleaning people, i was hoping that was
lemon pledge or something . . .

   they share a smile.

paint's not really a great thing to have in a museum.
people'll definitely take that the wrong way . . .

EVELYN

how do they know which way to take it?

ADAM

i'm thinking outside would be the general direction
they'd steer you with spray paint . . . why do you have
that?

EVELYN

i was going to do something to the nude. mess it up or . . . .

ADAM

what, you mean, like, colour it or something?

EVELYN

i was thinking more of painting a big dick on it, but
whatever . . .

ADAM

well, you could still colour it in . . . the dick.

evelyn smiles at this.

EVELYN

true. it might look kinda weird . . .

ADAM

oh, i think a graffiti penis is gonna be plenty odd already
. . . (*beat.*) so, right over the leaves there, or just a free-
floating number?

EVELYN

probably anatomically correct. i mean, if you're gonna
do it, why not . . .

ADAM

. . . do it right? absolutely. and, would 'why' be
completely out of the question here?

EVELYN

why the 'dick?'

ADAM

uh-huh. i mean, since i basically have to jump you now
if you lift that can up, it'd help with my report . . .

EVELYN

because i don't like art that isn't true.

ADAM

'true.' what do you mean?

EVELYN

false art. i hate it . . .

other patrons drift past. they watch them go.

ADAM

no, i understand the words you've used there, although
they're both pretty subjective: 'art.' 'truth.'

EVELYN

exactly! that's the beauty of art . . . it's subjective.

ADAM

right, but see, i don't know what you're referring to
then. i mean, specifically . . . (*beat.*) didn't oscar wilde
say something like, 'in art there is no such thing as a
universal truth . . .' or whatever?

EVELYN

yes . . . very good. 'a truth in art is that whose
contradictory is also true.' right, but that's an *aesthetic.*
i'm talking about practicalities. censorship. (*she points.*)
this sculpture. it's fake, it's not real. therefore, false art . . .

ADAM

no, it's a fornecelli, it definitely is. i read the little thingie
there one time . . .

EVELYN

yes, but the leaf cluster isn't.

ADAM

it's not? / what is it, a pastie or something, like strippers have?

EVELYN

no. / it's plaster . . . it was added by a committee who had complaints from local townspeople. / uh-huh. / they made a petition and got that put on, thereby removing its subjectivity as art.

ADAM

really? / i didn't know that . . . / when did they do this?

EVELYN

seven or eight years ago now, i think. before i got here, anyway. / see, they objected to his 'thing.' the shape of it. said it was too *life-like*. (*beat.*) it's supposed to be 'god,' you know . . . that's what pisses 'em off.

ADAM

huh. / yeah . . . he's not really supposed to have one of those, is he?

EVELYN

no, and i don't know why . . . we're always calling him 'the creator.' (*beat.*) look at it, you can see the . . . see right behind the grapes there, you can just see his . . .

ADAM

. . . grapes. yes. you're absolutely, huh. didn't even cover him properly. shoddy craftsmanship!

EVELYN

i mean, if you're gonna do it, at least . . .

ADAM

. . . exactly. do it right. (*beat.*) but why deface the thing?
i mean, just out of curiosity. why not, say, knock the
plaster off and expose his . . . you know . . . cluster . . .
if you're trying to . . .

EVELYN

because. that's so . . . expected.

ADAM

ahh . . . so, you're a student, then, or is this just basic
anarchy?

EVELYN

yep. student.

ADAM

me too.

EVELYN

yeah? what's your emphasis?

ADAM

ummm . . . taking out school loans, primarily, but i do
sit in on a few english classes. you're in art?

EVELYN

mmmm-hmmm. m.f.a. / applied theory and crit . . .

ADAM

oh. / so, is this, like, a project?

EVELYN

no, i'm just getting started on my thesis project now. a
big sorta installation . . . 'thingie.'

ADAM

that's a good word, huh? 'thingie.'

EVELYN

it is . . . (*points.*) anyway, *this* is only a pet peeve . . .

ADAM

thesis? you're graduating . . .

EVELYN

in may.

ADAM

'kay. i'm only a junior . . .

EVELYN

huh. you seem older.

ADAM

well, i am. i mean, older than twenty, anyhow . . .
i worked for a couple years. made money.

EVELYN

not enough, though. still got two jobs . . .

ADAM

don't forget the school loans . . .

EVELYN

right. so, basically, you're . . . fucked.

ADAM

yep. but at least i'm educated, so i *comprehend* that i'm
fucked . . .

they stand there for a moment. adam checks his watch;
evelyn shakes her spray can.

EVELYN

you're cute. i don't like the way you wear your hair . . .

ADAM

thank you. i think . . .

EVELYN

no, you're definitely cute, but you shouldn't style it so
much. your hair. just let it go . . .

ADAM

'kay. i'll try that . . .

EVELYN

your relief's late . . .

ADAM

yeah. typical . . .

EVELYN

so, do you have to stay at your station until they spell
you, or . . .?

ADAM

no, at punch-out time, i'm supposed to get down there
and do it. they can really be pricks about that . . .

EVELYN

you should go then . . .

ADAM

right. yeah, i . . . can i call you?

EVELYN

what do you wanna call me?

ADAM

up. just up, right now. talk, maybe get crazy, take you to
dinner . . .

EVELYN

okay. ahh . . . sure. (*beat.*) do they allow you to do that
here?

ADAM

what, eat dinner?

EVELYN

i meant hit on the patrons . . .

ADAM

. . . umm, no, they've got a pretty strict policy about
that, too, actually. but . . .

EVELYN

. . . ahh, the great equalizer. 'but.'

ADAM

exactly. i'll take the risk . . .

EVELYN

. . . good answer, grasshopper.

ADAM

huh?

EVELYN

'kung fu.' on tv. remember when he was a kid? the old
guy with the fakey contact lenses, and the . . .

ADAM

oh, right . . . sure. 'grasshopper.' i don't really watch much
television . . .

EVELYN

my brothers loved that show. (*beat.*) so, do you want a
number?

ADAM

absolutely! (*checks.*) damn, i don't have a pen.

EVELYN

me either. (*thinks.*) here . . .

ADAM

what?

EVELYN

the jacket. take it off for a second.

ADAM

oh, that's, umm . . .

EVELYN

what?

ADAM

it's my own . . . 's not part of the uniform. it's mine.

EVELYN

good. then you'll always have it on you . . . from the
looks of it.

> *adam follows her orders. evelyn lays the coat open on
> the floor, looks around, then uncaps the paint and
> sprays a phone number inside.*

. . . don't worry, it dries quick.

ADAM

thanks. okay, so, i'll . . . yeah. (*he glances back.*) good
luck with the . . . nice to meet you. again.

EVELYN

you too.

*adam smiles at her, looks back again, walks off.
evelyn is left alone. she turns back to the statue and
starts shaking her paint can. the little ball bearings
inside rattle loudly.*

adam standing with evelyn. he looks a bit different, not as bulky and he's letting his hair go. same jacket under his arm.

EVELYN

. . . no, seriously. you have.

ADAM

yeah?

EVELYN

no question.

ADAM

i dunno. i think i still look . . .

EVELYN

you can definitely tell. you can.

ADAM

really?

EVELYN

definitely. plus, the hair . . . / i bet you your friends say something. twenty bucks . . .

ADAM

well, i'm glad . . . / i mean, i can't tell and so i figured . . . twenty bucks?

EVELYN

yes. that's because you see 'you' every day. shower, getting dressed, that kind of thing. but . . .

ADAM

so do you.

EVELYN

i don't see you shower. or getting dressed . . .

ADAM

no, i meant every day. so far, anyway, since we first went
to . . .

EVELYN

i know, i'm kidding.

ADAM

oh. okay . . . (*beat.*) i'd like that, though. if you would . . .

EVELYN

which?

ADAM

both if you want. either. anything, any moment i can get
with you . . . that's what i'd like.

EVELYN

ask and you shall receive . . .

ADAM

so, i'm asking, then.

EVELYN

so you shall be receiving then . . .

   they share a brief kiss; he looks around self-
   consciously.

ADAM

p.d.a. public display of affection. i'm not used to that . . .

EVELYN

no? i don't mind . . .

ADAM

really?

EVELYN

nah, whose business is it? ours, right? kiss if we want to,
make love in the bathroom stall . . . who cares?

ADAM

i'd start with the management . . .

EVELYN

yeah, but why should they? i mean . . . we're two adults,
we . . .

ADAM

i think this is a bigger discussion than before jenny and
phillip get here . . . / i mean, no, i'd love to have it with
you, the discussion, and i agree, somewhat, but . . .

EVELYN

whatever. / i understand . . .

ADAM

another time, we'll definitely discuss it.

EVELYN

another time . . . i'd rather do it.

ADAM

lemme go check the men's room . . . (*he laughs.*) . . . you
amaze me.

EVELYN

i'm glad. (*beat.*) and *you* amaze *me*, you do. look at you!

ADAM

. . . it's just a little jogging.

EVELYN

no, it's not. it's not just that . . . you're running, you're
eating better, are you still lifting?

ADAM

yeah . . . i mean, i didn't today, but . . .

EVELYN

that's okay.

ADAM

no, i'm gonna . . . so, yeah, alright, it's a whole routine
thing. you're right . . .

EVELYN

do you like doing it?

ADAM

honestly . . . no. i totally hate it!

they laugh.

EVELYN

so why would you . . . ?

ADAM

because you suggested it. which is kinda pathetic, but
true . . .

EVELYN

you shouldn't do something you don't wanna do.

ADAM

yeah, you should, why not? if it's for someone . . . i mean, i'm doing it for you.

EVELYN

it's a life change. really . . .

ADAM

right.

EVELYN

i gave you a couple ideas and you're changing your entire life. i'm very proud of you.

ADAM

thank you . . . (*cockney*) . . . 'enry 'iggins.

EVELYN

what's that? who's . . .

ADAM

nothing. from a book. play, actually.

EVELYN

oh. (*beat.*) are you keeping your journal? it really does help . . .

ADAM

yes.

EVELYN

will you let me read it?

ADAM

. . . some time.

EVELYN

good.

they stand for a moment. evelyn checks her watch.

ADAM

and what about you?

EVELYN

what about me?

ADAM

that's what i mean . . . i don't know.

EVELYN

what?

ADAM

nothing. i don't really know anything about you . . .

EVELYN

yes, you do!

ADAM

i don't. not really . . .

EVELYN

what's my name?

ADAM

evelyn.

EVELYN

where am i from?

ADAM

illinois. near chicago?

EVELYN

yes. how old am i?

ADAM

ummm . . . twenty-five, maybe.

EVELYN

that's exactly right. almost twenty-six. sign?

ADAM

gemini, i think . . .

EVELYN

the twins, yes.

ADAM

does that mean you have a split personality?

EVELYN

no, it means i was born in june.

ADAM

oh. (*beat*.) and you're, what, a sculptress, right? an
artist . . .

EVELYN

yep. anything else you wanna know?

ADAM

yes . . . everything!

EVELYN

so ask then . . .

ADAM

well . . . why are you always asking me questions if it's
no big deal.

EVELYN

because you make me curious . . . i'm a curious person.

ADAM

i'm curious, too, though!

EVELYN

like i said . . . so ask then.

ADAM

. . . why do you like me?

EVELYN

what?

ADAM

me . . . why would you like me? i'm not anything,
i mean . . . and you're so . . .

EVELYN

don't do that, okay? that's the only thing about you
i don't like . . . what you see in yourself. or don't see.
your insecurities. (*beat.*) do you like me?

ADAM

of course, you know i do . . .

EVELYN

do i appear to like you? hmm?

ADAM

yes . . . it seems like it, yeah.

EVELYN

i *do* like you. do you think i'm smart?

ADAM

i think you're amazing . . . and you have a *great* ass. just
thought you should know . . .

EVELYN

not part of my query, but thank you.

ADAM

welcome . . .

EVELYN

and do i seem to know my own mind? i mean,
generally . . .

ADAM

no question.

EVELYN

so, don't you trust me, then, to know how i feel?

ADAM

yeah. no, you're right . . .

EVELYN

don't worry about *why* when *what* is right in front of you.

ADAM

those're very wise words from someone with such a
great ass . . .

EVELYN

(*playfully*) kiss me, grasshopper . . .

they start to kiss again as a young couple approaches.

JENNY

ah, ah, ah . . . p.d.a.

PHILLIP

i don't think anybody wants to watch you kiss, adam . . . we'll be eating soon.

ADAM

hey, phillip, hello! evelyn, this is phillip, and his fiancée, jenny . . .

'hellos' all round.

PHILLIP

so, we should grab a table, and . . . *(stopping to look)* adam, what's up with you? d'you lost weight?

ADAM

. . . a little, maybe.

JENNY

no, he cut his hair . . . or something. that's it, right?

ADAM

umm, yeah. i mean, both, sort of.

PHILLIP

huh. okay, so, let's . . . come on.

jenny and phillip lead the way. evelyn stares at adam as they follow; he pulls a twenty out of his pocket and places it in her hand.

A LIVING ROOM

adam and evelyn sitting on a couch. jenny and phillip in opposing chairs. everyone holds a drink.

ADAM

. . . so, tell me this again, you're going to what?

PHILLIP

underwater. we're going to get married underwater . . .

ADAM

you've gotta be kidding me!

PHILLIP

. . . like those *life* magazine photos you see or whatever. seriously.

JENNY

we wanted to try something bold . . .

EVELYN

that oughta do it.

ADAM

this is crazy, really. and, so, if we want to attend we have to . . .

PHILLIP

. . . get in the tank with us. you bet.

JENNY

no, honey, i thought we said . . .

PHILLIP

. . . we haven't, okay, no, we haven't settled that part
completely, but . . .

JENNY

my dad could never do that. i mean, my mom would try,
she would, but dad . . .

PHILLIP

maybe people can watch from the glass window things
or whatever, but i'd prefer if they came in with us . . .
(*he drains his glass, looking at adam.*)

ADAM

that is nuts . . .

EVELYN

i applaud you. i think it's very . . .

PHILLIP

(*to evelyn*) yeah, well, don't expect my buddy here to
follow in our footsteps. he's the least adventurous person
i know . . .

EVELYN

really?

PHILLIP

absolutely! and the marriage thing? uh-uh, not gonna
happen, sorry. i don't know how many nights i listened
to this guy say, 'not me, man, i'm never getting hooked,
no way, man . . .'

EVELYN

is that right? well, well . . .

ADAM

listen, don't encourage him. my room-mate doesn't need
any . . .

PHILLIP

. . . former room-mate . . .

ADAM

. . . more encouragement. (*beat.*) i'm gonna look stupid
in one of those wet suits.

PHILLIP

hey, let's not be a party-pooper here, my friend . . . this
could've been you.

adam laughs thinly; evelyn doesn't understand.

ADAM

i know, i know . . .

PHILLIP

right?

EVELYN

i'm lost. what's . . .?

PHILLIP

i stole jenny away from adam . . .

ADAM

come on . . .

PHILLIP

i did! (*to jenny*) didn't i?

JENNY

no, you didn't, stop being . . . (*to evelyn*) adam and i had
a class together, but he never got up the nerve to ask me
out.

EVELYN

is that true?

ADAM

something like that . . .

JENNY

four months we sat next to each other – i'm borrowing
his pen, like, all the time, hint-hint – and he's this total
monk the whole semester . . . anyway, phil picks him up
from class one day, sees me, and we went to the movies
that same night.

PHILLIP

i cannot tell a lie . . . i've got the moves, god help me.

ADAM

god help all of us . . .

   a collective laugh.

EVELYN

well, like i said, i think it's great. it's really amazing, it is,
to find anybody willing to take a risk today. to look a
little silly or different or anything. bravo! (*toasts.*) to
people with balls . . .

   *they all toast, even phillip with his empty glass, but he
   looks over at adam. adam blushes.*

PHILLIP

'balls,' huh? yep, that's my jenny . . .

jenny slaps him on the shoulder and blushes again.

EVELYN

you know what i mean. guts. that kinda thing . . .

JENNY

right. i got it.

PHILLIP

(*toasting*) 'to balls, long may they wave . . .'

they all smile and 'mock' drink again.

i'll tell you what took some balls, the museum thing, a few weeks back, with the . . . balls. you guys read about that?! i mean, adam, of course you did, you work there, but – evelyn, you hear about it?

JENNY

(*whispering*) the penis . . .

EVELYN

(*whispering*) yes, i did. why are we whispering?

PHILLIP

because you don't say 'penis' in jenny's house. but we're at my place now, and so we sing it from the eaves! 'penis!! pe-nis!!!'

ADAM

okay, bar's closing, last call . . .

EVELYN

i'm an artist, so i didn't . . .

PHILLIP

no, seriously, do you believe that shit? somebody with
the gall to do that kinda bullshit on our campus?! that
fucking burns me up . . .

ADAM

we should probably get, umm . . .

PHILLIP

. . . what does that mean, anyway? 'i'm an artist?'

EVELYN

it means nothing, really, just that i understand the
impulse . . .

PHILLIP

you what?!

ADAM

evelyn, maybe we should . . .

PHILLIP

no, wait adam, i wanna hear . . . what 'impulse?' it's
called 'vandalism.'

JENNY

does anyone want dessert?

*phillip holds up a hand to hush the group. he turns
back to evelyn.*

PHILLIP

no, hold on, this is rich. go ahead . . .

EVELYN

just that . . . i don't think it was just kids playing. i think
it was a sort of statement, a kind of . . .

PHILLIP

. . . a statement?

EVELYN

yeah, i do . . .

JENNY

what kind of statement would that be? it was
pornography . . .

EVELYN

no, it wasn't.

JENNY

yes, it was . . .

EVELYN

pornography is meant to titillate, to excite you. did you
see a picture of what happened?

PHILLIP

we did, yeah . . .

EVELYN

does a penis excite you? i mean, just any ol' penis?

PHILLIP

you're funny. and that's not the point.

EVELYN

it's totally the point . . . how about you, jenny, did you
like what you saw? did it get you hot?

PHILLIP

this is, like, uncalled for, okay? all she said was . . .

EVELYN

i know what she said, why don't you let her speak?
(*to jenny*) did you wanna say anything else? huh? okay,
then . . . all i'm saying is that, in my *opinion*, it wasn't
pornography, it was a statement. of course, that's the
beauty of statements, like art, they're subjective. you and
i can think completely different things and we can both
be right . . . unless, and this seems quite probable, you
just can't stand to lose an argument.

quiet for a moment from the group.

PHILLIP

wow. the postgraduate mind at work . . .

ADAM

i'll help you get dessert, jenny, if you want to . . .

JENNY

. . . i still don't think that makes it a statement. it's
graffiti . . .

EVELYN

what do you mean, it would be a huge statement . . .
especially for a town like this.

PHILLIP

hey, some of us are from 'a town like this,' so maybe you
should watch it.

EVELYN

well, we've all gotta be from somewhere . . .

PHILLIP

what do you mean by that?

EVELYN

i mean, it's a little college town in the middle of nowhere
and . . .

PHILLIP

one you chose, presumably . . .

EVELYN

no, it chose me, actually. *full* scholarship. so, as i was
saying . . .

PHILLIP

you've got a real winning way, you know that?

ADAM

look, phil, it's no big deal, let's just . . .

PHILLIP

which 'take back the night' rally did you find her at,
adam?

EVELYN

. . . can i finish, please?! jesus, you're really the
obnoxious type, you know that? (*to adam*) how long
did you have to stomach this guy?

everyone except evelyn sort of freezes on that one.

ADAM

evelyn.

EVELYN

anyhow, who knows what the person was saying by it,
we don't, but i think it was a gesture. a kind of manifesto,
if you will . . .

PHILLIP

(*dryly*) i don't think a person's dick can be a manifesto.
uh-uh. you can write a manifesto on your thing, but
your thing can't be one . . . i'm sure i read that
somewhere.

EVELYN

see? you're just trying to be . . .

PHILLIP

i'm not trying to be anything! who the hell do you think
you are, a few double dates and telling me anything
about who i am? un-fucking-believable!

JENNY

this is getting a little, ahh . . .

PHILLIP

. . . adam, you can really pick 'em. wow, man!

ADAM

look, it's not, let's just forget the . . .

EVELYN

you're not gonna take his side in this, are you?

ADAM

i'm not taking sides, i'm trying to get outta here with
just a touch of dignity, okay? jesus . . .

JENNY

i've got a test tomorrow, anyway . . .

PHILLIP

'statement,' she says!

EVELYN

shut the fuck up, alright? just fuck right off . . . how
would you know? i think she was making one, so that's
my opinion . . .

ADAM

jenny, thanks for everything. phillip, i'll call ya, or
whatever, but we're gonna . . .

PHILLIP

yeah? how do you know it was a girl?

EVELYN

. . . i don't. i didn't say it was a woman.

PHILLIP

girl, woman, whatever. you said 'she,' how do you know
that?

EVELYN

i don't, i just said. it's a guess. what it was, where it was
placed. an *educated* guess . . .

PHILLIP

you are not . . . she's not trying to take a poke at my
being an undergrad, is she? adam, tell me she didn't
just . . .

JENNY

can we stop, now, please?! you guys . . .

ADAM

evelyn, let's go . . .

PHILLIP

hey, artiste . . . how'd you know it was a woman who
painted the cock, huh? very, very suspicious there . . .

EVELYN

you are such a prick, man, how do you go on, day after
day? (*to adam*) let's go . . . (*she rises, snatches up her
things and moves toward the door.*) adam? are you
coming?

ADAM

i'm . . . yeah, but, just go. i'll meet you downstairs, i just
wanna . . . go ahead.

EVELYN

'kay. (*to jenny*) you're very sweet. good luck . . . i don't
think that's gonna be enough, but i still wish it on you.
    she heads for the door and exits.

PHILLIP

'good luck.' hey, fuck. you! (*to adam*) where in hell did
you meet that bitch?! / what'd she do, give you a haircut
and a blow job and now you're her puppy?!! / you don't
have to go . . .

ADAM

. . . at the museum. / no, i'm not her . . . (*to jenny*) the
wedding sounds great. really . . . it sounds . . . yeah.

    he wanders off. phillip and jenny sit in silence.

PHILLIP

. . . what?

A BEDROOM

*adam and evelyn in bed. holding each other, staring off.
a video camera on a tripod nearby.*

EVELYN

. . . umm, nice.

ADAM

very. yes.

EVELYN

our bodies are beginning to understand one another . . .

ADAM

you're right, i mean . . .

EVELYN

getting a rhythm. and less inhibited.

ADAM

yep.

*he leans over and whispers something in her ear.
a huge smile across her face. she turns and whispers
back to him. they laugh and kiss for a moment.
they hold one another.*

EVELYN

(*quietly*) were you always like this before? so . . . you
know . . .

ADAM

. . . shy? just about the fact that no one would sleep with
me. that's all.

EVELYN

come on . . .

ADAM

seriously. you're only, like, i dunno, the third person i've
ever . . .

EVELYN

. . . no . . .

ADAM

yes, i mean it. and they were both young. i mean, i was
too, i wasn't, like, hanging out at a *day care* or anything,
but . . . it was during high school mostly. so . . . you're
sort of in uncharted waters here.

EVELYN

i don't wanna blow your cover but . . . i could kinda tell.

ADAM

(*smiling*) yeah? well, that's okay . . .

EVELYN

and nobody here at school?

ADAM

nothing serious. dates. some close calls. but not anyone . . .
you know.

EVELYN

. . . like jenny.

ADAM

no.

EVELYN

you sorry you didn't ask her out? i mean, if i wasn't in
the equation . . .

ADAM

not really. we just never got the right . . . whatever.
i sorta blew that one. anyway, it's kind of weird talking
about . . .

EVELYN

it's okay. that's nice to see, every so often. someone
gallant . . .

ADAM

which is medieval for 'loser' . . . (*beat*.) i wanna tell you
something – and this is not because we've been sleeping
together or because you mentioned another girl, it's not –
i can't stop thinking about you. i can't. i mean, it's not
like a stalker situation . . . yet . . . but i'm finding myself
hanging out by your classes. following you . . .

EVELYN

i've noticed . . .

ADAM

i figured, yeah. and taking my jacket off, like, thirty
times a day and looking at your number. staring at it.
wondering if you're looking at my number. and writing
your name on anything! all over my books. in my *food*.
seriously, tracing your name in whatever i'm eating. i'm
so whipped . . . you are dangerously close to owning me.

EVELYN

wow . . .

ADAM

i just signed my relationship death warrant, didn't i?
what a dork . . .

EVELYN

. . . no, it's sweet. (*beat.*) were you nervous tonight? i
mean, about us with the . . .

ADAM

nah. not really. a bit.

EVELYN

sure?

ADAM

yeah. it's just . . . let's not watch it, okay? do we have to
do that?

EVELYN

not if you don't want to . . .

ADAM

good. i don't think i could get into that, actually . . .

EVELYN

why not? it'd be fun . . .

ADAM

i don't really need to see myself doing that. doing . . .
stuff.

EVELYN

see, i'm totally different. i think everyone should see
themselves doing it, and their friends should see it, too.

ADAM

and that's why the tape's gonna stay at my place . . .

she smiles at this, kissing him.

EVELYN

don't be so frightened of everything.

ADAM

i'm not. not frightened, anyway. i just don't think that's a thing other people need to see. ever. my ass . . .

EVELYN

people like who . . . phillip?

ADAM

no, that's fine, you can show it to him . . . (*beat.*) are you nuts?!

EVELYN

why is he your friend?

ADAM

do you really wanna go over that . . .?

EVELYN

i just don't get it.

ADAM

what's to get? we were room-mates, we occasionally see each other, have a drink . . .

EVELYN

i just don't think you need that kind of person in your life. no one does.

ADAM

(*mock-serious*) . . . it may be a touch early to start dictating who my friends are.

EVELYN

(*with charm*) yeah . . . i s'pose.

ADAM

geez, he really got under your skin, didn't he?

EVELYN

under. over. around. i hate that kind of guy . . .

ADAM

what kind?

EVELYN

that kind. whatever he is, that's what i hate . . .

ADAM

i'll let him know.

EVELYN

no, god, no, don't give him the satisfaction. and he'd take it, too, believe me . . .

ADAM

nah, maybe it'd help him, you know, be better . . . or something.

EVELYN

the only thing that would help him is a fucking knife through his throat . . .

they grow quiet for a moment. adam studies evelyn.

ADAM

okay, i'm glad i don't have a pet rabbit or anything right
now . . .

EVELYN

(*laughing*) you know what i mean.

ADAM

ummmm, no, not really.

EVELYN

i've just been around his type, that's all. and i don't like
'em.

ADAM

yeah, i got that part . . .

EVELYN

no big deal.

ADAM

right, no, it was the 'knife through the throat' part that
was the big deal, i thought . . .

EVELYN

oh, that's just an expression.

ADAM

. . . from where, transylvania?

   she kisses him.

EVELYN

no . . . from the 'scorned girl's handbook.'

ADAM

ahhh. right . . . page 666.

EVELYN

(*smiling*) you've been peeking. you know what happens
to peekers, don't you?

ADAM

well, if they're d.j.s, they usually get asked to play 'misty'
on the radio all the time . . .

EVELYN

close. no, i'll show you . . . but you have to do me a
favour.

ADAM

what's that?

   she starts to slip under the covers.

EVELYN

. . . just smile. smile into the camera. for as long as you
can . . .

A PARK

*jenny waiting on a bench. sitting by herself. after a
moment, adam appears.*

ADAM

. . . hey.

JENNY

adam, hi, hello.

ADAM

hi.

JENNY

thanks for coming, i appreciate it.

ADAM

of course. how's it going?

JENNY

you know . . . okay.

ADAM

right.

JENNY

lots to do for a wedding.

ADAM

i'll bet . . .

JENNY

invitations to get out, arrangements to make . . .

ADAM

. . . air tanks to fill . . .

jenny laughs lightly.

JENNY

that too.

ADAM

so, you guys're still going through with that?

JENNY

that's what we're saying . . .

ADAM

what do you mean, 'saying?'

JENNY

no, we are, it's what we're doing, i'm just . . .

ADAM

. . . jenny, what?

JENNY

i don't know. i'm, you know, worried.

ADAM

why? about what?

JENNY

what do you think? phillip. he's just . . . i dunno, being
funny.

ADAM

funny, how? like 'telling jokes' funny or 'making letter
bombs' funny?

JENNY

no, no bombs yet, but kind of . . . just funny. odd.
(*beat.*) like, nice . . .

ADAM

'nice?'

JENNY

yeah, you know . . . sweet. now, i love him and all, i do,
you know that, but that's not the way i'd describe him to
people. 'sweet.' would you?

adam thinks for a moment.

ADAM

no, i wouldn't exactly use his name and 'sweet' in the
same short story . . .

JENNY

and that's what's bugging me.

ADAM

why, though? maybe he's just . . .

JENNY

i've only seen him like this once before, maybe twice.
definitely once, when we were first going out and he was
seeing somebody else, too. it was over, mostly, but he
was still seeing her. remember that?

ADAM

. . . yeah. i do. the 'other' one.

JENNY

the other jenny, exactly. i'd call and i could hear him
freeze up, stop for a moment if he answered and i said,

'hey, it's jenny.' he didn't know what to do, so he'd get all sort of sweet and fish around slowly until he figured out if it was her or me . . . god, i used to hate that!

ADAM

so, do you know anyone else named 'jenny' right now?

JENNY

no, i don't mean that, not the name so much as the feeling . . . that sense that there's someone else.

ADAM

nah . . .

JENNY

maybe i'm making it up, you know, my own insecurities and looking for a reason to not . . .

ADAM

(*smiling*) . . . dive in? take the plunge? jump off the deep end? stop me before i . . .

JENNY

cute . . . but yes. and that might be it, but i don't think so. i want to get married, i do, and i love the guy, whether he's sweet or not. it's just that i don't believe him now that he is . . .

ADAM

well, you got me . . .

JENNY

really? you don't know anything, haven't felt that or . . .

ADAM

i only see him, like, once a week in our survey course, so it's not like i'm in the inner circle any more . . .

JENNY

i know, i just thought that . . .

ADAM

. . . but i would tell you, jenny, i would, seriously.

JENNY

really?

ADAM

i think so . . . i mean, that's a lousy thing to pass on to a person, and if i did, you know, know something and then told you, you'd more likely hate me for ever than be grateful . . .

JENNY

yeah, that's probably true . . .

ADAM

ummm, you could lie, you know, feel free.

JENNY

no, you're probably right . . .

ADAM

so, that doesn't exactly make me want to come clean here – which i don't have anything to come clean about, okay, honestly, i just mean, whatever – but i feel i would. i do, because i think you're pretty amazing, if the truth be known, and you're almost married so why shouldn't it be? the truth, i mean.

JENNY

. . . thank you.

ADAM

not a problem. anyway, that's all i know. which is,
nothing . . .

JENNY

'kay. i'm just being stupid.

ADAM

look, if you feel it, it's not stupid . . .

jenny studies him hard.

JENNY

you're a lovely person, you know that?

ADAM

'lovely?' jesus, why don't you just call me 'gay' and get
it over with?

JENNY

hey, 'lovely' is nice . . . i wish there were a few more
'lovely' people in the world. i mean it, you are. (*looks
at him again.*) and getting cuter by the day. what is that
girl doing to you?

ADAM

lots . . . she's amazing, really.

JENNY

what happened to your . . . are you wearing . . . adam,
are those contacts?

ADAM

yeah. contacts.

JENNY

my god, this from the former 'tape around the nose
thing-y' champion . . .

ADAM

that was only for a week, that one time!

JENNY

still, you've gotta admit . . .

ADAM

i do, it's amazing. i feel better . . .

JENNY

better? you're, like, this totally hot guy now . . . (*beat.*)
i always thought you were handsome, anyway, but
i didn't think you'd go in for the makeover thing.

ADAM

me either. who knew?

JENNY

well, apparently she did . . . (*beat.*) you are still seeing
her, aren't you?

ADAM

oh yeah. she's . . . you don't hold a grudge, all she said
that night at your . . . god, i couldn't believe that!

JENNY

it was great. no, truthfully, it was, phil needed to hear
every word of that and he did, too. hear it, i mean. even
said something after you guys left that night. not an
admittance of guilt, exactly, but as close to one as we're
likely to hear from the guy . . .

ADAM

really, what'd he say? i'm amazed . . .

JENNY

as was i . . . he put on quite the show . . .

ADAM

(*sarcastically*) yeah, i remember vaguely . . . they both
did.

JENNY

right, but later he said something like, 'he could do
worse.'

ADAM

not exactly a seal of approval . . .

JENNY

no, but a lot. for him. and after what she said . . .

ADAM

you're right. huh.

JENNY

hey . . . her middle name's not 'jenny' or anything, is it?

   adam laughs at this.

ADAM

nah, no such luck. it's 'ann.' evelyn ann thompson. nice,
right?

JENNY

eat.

ADAM

huh?

JENNY

'eat.' those're her initials, the acronym of her names.
e-a-t.

ADAM

hey, that's cute . . .

JENNY

oh god, you're a goner.

ADAM

i know, it's pathetic, isn't it?

JENNY

yeah, somewhat . . . but lovely.

ADAM

not that again . . .

*he puts a hand up to hide his face. jenny grabs one of
his hands, studying it.*

JENNY

what the heck is this? what is this?!

ADAM

what . . .?

JENNY

did you stop biting your nails?

ADAM

yeah, for, like, a month now . . .

JENNY

don't tell me . . .

ADAM

it's true. she put some crap on them, slapped 'em out of
my mouth a few times and that was it. i stopped . . .

JENNY

you have nails! this is crazy . . .

ADAM

it's no big . . .

JENNY

ever since i've known you, three years now, your
fingers've looked like raw meat . . . anyway, awful. and
now you just quit?! this girl is the messiah.

ADAM

i've quit before . . .

JENNY

for, like, an hour! (*beat.*) i love this woman . . .

ADAM

me too.

JENNY

yeah, i see that. wow . . .

she looks over at adam again.

and you'd really tell me if you knew something?

ADAM

. . . i would. yes.

JENNY

'kay. damn, when did you get so cute?

55

she kisses him lightly on the cheek. they look at each other for a long moment. suddenly, they kiss. a real kiss, not a 'great to see you, aren't we the best of friends' kiss. after a moment, they shudder to a halt.

ADAM

. . . shit.

JENNY

yeah. huh.

ADAM

what was that all about?

JENNY

i dunno. i just . . . i'm not sure.

ADAM

look, i'm sorry.

JENNY

no, don't be. i am. i'm the one with the ring on . . .

ADAM

yeah, good point. my friend's ring. thanks for reminding me . . .

JENNY

welcome.

ADAM

oh, god . . . damn it!

JENNY

. . . no, listen. it wasn't because of, you know, my worries or whatever. how i feel about phillip right now. it wasn't . . .

ADAM

okay.

JENNY

it just . . .

ADAM

. . . happened.

JENNY

right. i've wanted to do that for a long time . . . three
years . . .

ADAM

. . . me too. (*beat.*) and now we take it out in the woods
and bury it . . . don't we?

JENNY

yeah. i mean, yes, definitely. i guess . . .

ADAM

don't you think? we have to . . . jesus, what're we even
talking about?!

JENNY

no, we do. 'course. don't you want to?

ADAM

bury it?

JENNY

yes . . . or . . .

ADAM

no, we can't talk about . . . don't even say the . . . do you
have a shovel in your car?

JENNY

i don't, no . . . but i have my car.

ADAM

. . . my bike's right over there.

JENNY

is it locked up?

ADAM

uh-huh.

JENNY

then it should be fine . . .

ADAM

i suppose so. it's a small town, after all.

JENNY

that's what people say . . .

ADAM

good people. people we know and care about . . .

JENNY

right. (*beat*.) come on, we should go bury this. out in the
woods . . .

*they kiss again, then stand up slowly and walk off.
she puts an arm through his.*

*adam and evelyn sit on opposing couches, flipping
through magazines. after a moment, he glances up and
checks his watch.*

ADAM

what time did they say?

EVELYN

like, ten-thirty . . .

ADAM

and it's ten-fifty now . . .

EVELYN

no big deal, you always wait at the doctor's office.

ADAM

i know, i just have to be at work by twelve.

EVELYN

today?

ADAM

yeah, i told you that . . .

EVELYN

no, you didn't.

ADAM

i did . . . i always work wednesdays.

EVELYN

really?

ADAM

yeah, every wednesday.

EVELYN

damn. i hope they . . .

ADAM

it's okay. i guess i could be a little late if i have to . . .

EVELYN

sure?

ADAM

uh-huh. it's alright . . . i mean, they hate it but i can
make something up.

EVELYN

we can go.

ADAM

no, i wanna do this. i do . . . (*beat.*) who wouldn't want
to get their nose chopped off?

EVELYN

come on! it's not . . .

ADAM

i'm kidding. no, i think you're right about it . . .

EVELYN

it's just shaving it . . .

ADAM

yeah, that's much better. 'shaving' your nose off . . . that
settles the nerves.

EVELYN

you're only talking to them, anyway, that's all.

ADAM

i know, it's just weird to think . . .

EVELYN

people do it all the time.

ADAM

right, no, you're right, i just never imagined myself one
of those people . . .

EVELYN

i'm one of those people. would you ever've guessed that?

ADAM

what? you are not . . .

EVELYN

bullshit. take a look . . .

ADAM

where . . . ?

he moves over to her, studies her nose.

i don't see anything.

EVELYN

exactly.

ADAM

you had your nose done? honestly?

EVELYN

at sixteen. my parents' birthday present . . .

ADAM

thoughtful . . .

EVELYN

no, i asked for it. i had this terrible hook. 'the jewish
slope,' we called it in lake forest . . . the only ski run for
miles around!

ADAM

(*smiling*) i can't believe it . . . i can't tell . . .

EVELYN

that's the idea, isn't it?

ADAM

yeah, but . . . you could be lying to me.

EVELYN

and what would be the point of that?

ADAM

to get me in here. to watch chunks of my flesh get torn
away . . . you could be a sadist, for all i know . . .

EVELYN

hey, quit sweet-talking me . . .

ADAM

well, they did an amazing job. (*beat.*) wait a minute,
your name's 'thompson,' that's not jewish . . .

EVELYN

on my mother's side, you dope. that's what makes me
jewish . . . her maiden name is 'tessman.'

ADAM

oh.

EVELYN

we don't have to stay here, adam . . .

ADAM

no, it's alright, it just makes me a little jumpy . . .

EVELYN

it's cosmetic, not corrective . . . it's no big deal. i
promise . . .

ADAM

if it's cosmetic, why can't i just put some powder on it or
something, or shade it in on the side like they do for
richard gere in photos . . .

EVELYN

you mean, before?

ADAM

. . . he had it done?!

EVELYN

take a look at *american gigolo* and then at any picture
of him today. i'm serious. lots of guys do it . . . joel grey.

ADAM

okay, that's it, let's go . . .

EVELYN

(*laughing*) kidding! what about sting?

ADAM

yeah, i knew he did. looked totally different in
quadrophenia. i used to rent that video all the time, my
'mod' phase . . .

EVELYN

that must've been cute . . . (*beat.*) does he look better
now? sting, i mean?

ADAM

i suppose so . . . maybe it's just all that yoga, though.

EVELYN

i think you'll look great. you have a good face, a nice
shape to your nose, actually, but it's just got that bit
of . . .

ADAM

what?

EVELYN

. . . bulb . . . at the end. not a bulb, exactly, but . . .

ADAM

no, i got it, sort of the 'rudolph' effect. at least i can
guide your sleigh tonight . . .

EVELYN

you can guide my sleigh any night.

they look at one another, kiss.

ADAM

p.d.a.

EVELYN

indeed . . .

ADAM

shall i check the men's room?

EVELYN

i dare you . . .

ADAM

shut up!

EVELYN

i'm serious . . .

ADAM

you're crazy . . .

EVELYN

quite possibly. i still dare you . . .

ADAM

what if they call us?

EVELYN

then they'll just have to wait, won't they?

ADAM

i suppose they would . . .

EVELYN

can you afford to be late, that's the question. will you
take the risk . . .?

ADAM

is this, like, my last meal or something? a conjugal visit
before i'm drawn and quartered . . .

EVELYN

stop being so morbid . . . it's just flesh.

ADAM

yeah, i see what you mean . . . 'it's just flesh,' that's not
morbid at all.

EVELYN

it isn't. it's one of the most perfect substances on earth.
natural, beautiful. think about it . . .

ADAM

i'd rather not.

EVELYN

oh come on . . . you've bitten more skin off from around
your fingernails than a doctor would ever trim off your
nose. it's true . . .

ADAM

yeah, but that's just . . .

EVELYN

. . . what? it's the same thing. now, that grows back and
this wouldn't, but that's about the only difference. (*beat.*)
how did you get that scar on your back?

ADAM

which, the . . .?

EVELYN

yes. the raised one . . .

ADAM

a kid, umm, threw a stick at me . . . first grade.

EVELYN

stitches?

ADAM

yeah. thirty-three . . .

EVELYN

and is that terrible? are you disfigured because of it . . .?

ADAM

well, i don't like to wear tanktops . . .

EVELYN

. . . and you should be respected for that . . .

ADAM

(*giggling*) i'm serious . . . it bugs me . . .

EVELYN

okay, but why? because it looks ugly or because you
think other people will think it looks bad? which?

ADAM

i dunno . . .

EVELYN

what's the matter with scars? not a thing . . . (*pulls up
sleeve.*) look at these, see there?

ADAM

what're those?

EVELYN

they're scars . . . lots of little scars. you didn't notice
them before?

ADAM

yeah, i guess i did, but i didn't think anything . . .

EVELYN

sure, you did. of course you would, they're on my wrist.
you know what they are . . .

ADAM

. . . did you try to . . .?

EVELYN

no, not really. i mean, i cut on myself a little, tried to get
attention when i was a teenager, but i didn't want to slit
my veins open. or i would have . . .

ADAM

oh.

EVELYN

i'm a very straightforward person.

ADAM

yeah, i'm getting that . . .

EVELYN

it's the only way to be. why lie?

ADAM

you're right.

EVELYN

exactly. (*beat*.) so, is my arm unattractive to you, then,
because of those, or not? tell me . . .

ADAM

no . . .

EVELYN

are you lying?

ADAM

no, not at all, i love your arm.

EVELYN

'love' is a big word . . .

ADAM

i know that, that's why i used it, i don't throw it around,
believe me . . .

EVELYN

neither do i.

ADAM

i love your arm. it's beautiful . . . (*he takes hold of her
wrist gently, kisses it.*)

EVELYN

they're like rings on a tree. they signify experience . . .
make us unique.

ADAM

i can see that.

EVELYN

and that's all this is, the idea of you having some surgery.
it's an experience . . .

ADAM

i know, it just makes me . . .

EVELYN

. . . what, nervous? of course you should be nervous,
why not? it's something you've never done . . . but that's
the adventure.

ADAM

'it's a far, far better thing i do than i have ever done . . .'

EVELYN

something like that. is that from a book?

ADAM

yeah, dickens . . .

EVELYN

huh. well, i don't know about better, but at least
different.

   another quick kiss.

so, are you gonna go check?

ADAM

what? . . . you mean, the rest room?

EVELYN

uh-huh.

ADAM

ummm . . . okay. what if they call my name, though?
seriously . . .

EVELYN

what if they do?

ADAM

(*smiling*) i smell trouble . . . which i may not be able to
do after this.

EVELYN

just go . . .

ADAM

(*standing*) okay, why not? then i can show you
something . . .

EVELYN

what?

ADAM

just a little thing i had done. for you.

EVELYN

wait, what . . . show me now.

*he looks around, can't wait. he pulls open his pants
and lets her glance inside.*

ADAM

look . . . a big religious no-no. (*pulls at his waistband.*)
nice, huh?

EVELYN

'eat.' lemme guess . . . you couldn't afford the 'me.'

ADAM

no, you goof! your *initials*. like it?

EVELYN

(*touching it*) i do, i like it. and i love the gesture . . .

ADAM

'love' is a big word.

EVELYN

i know that. that's why i used it . . . (*beat.*) go check the
'handicapped' stall. i'm suddenly very hungry . . .

*he slips off, out of the waiting room. evelyn goes back
to reading her magazine, when a voice calls out.*

VOICE

mr sorenson. adam sorenson, please . . .

*evelyn looks up, glances toward where adam has
disappeared but says nothing. she smiles.*

A LAWN

phillip and adam sitting on their jackets between classes,
talking. adam has a bandage across his nose.

PHILLIP

i'm serious, it looks good . . .

ADAM

just shut up . . . don't get here late and then make fun of
me.

PHILLIP

no, you look distinguished.

ADAM

phil, i look like a hockey player . . .

PHILLIP

yeah, but a distinguished one.

   they chuckle.

what'd you do, anyway?

ADAM

. . . i fell.

PHILLIP

come on . . .

ADAM

seriously, i did . . .

PHILLIP

you sound like a battered wife. 'i fell . . .'

ADAM

that's not funny.

PHILLIP

yeah, it is . . . it's very funny. i mean, it's not that funny
that wives get beat up, but the fact that you look like
one, that i find hilarious . . .

ADAM

well, anyway, that's what happened. i tripped, i fell . . .
no big deal.

PHILLIP

sure it wasn't the bathroom door? that's the usual
excuse . . .

ADAM

for who?

PHILLIP

abused women . . .

ADAM

you're sick.

PHILLIP

somewhat, yeah. but i'm nice-looking, which makes up
for a lot.

ADAM

not as much as you think . . .

PHILLIP

'don't hate me because i'm beautiful.'

ADAM

i don't . . . i just hate you.

PHILLIP

see, i knew you did, all these years . . . (*beat.*) you really
fell?

ADAM

yeah. i tripped on the stairs going into my apartment and
caught my face on the . . . you know . . . the . . .

PHILLIP

no, what?

ADAM

oh, come on! it's not that fascinating . . .

PHILLIP

it is, too. it's completely fascinating. so, you don't wanna
tell me then, right?

ADAM

tell you what?!

PHILLIP

what happened to your . . .

ADAM

i told you. i tripped going up the . . . and hit the edge of
the . . .

PHILLIP

yeah, it's the 'edge of' that i'm a little hazy on here . . .

ADAM

edge of the knob. my door knob.

PHILLIP

she clocked you one, didn't she?

ADAM

who?

PHILLIP

'who?' the artist, formerly known as evelyn, or whatever
her name is . . .

ADAM

are you nuts?

PHILLIP

well, i've gotta hand it to her, she certainly made a
'statement' . . .

ADAM

you are such an idiot . . .

PHILLIP

did she hit you?

ADAM

stop!

PHILLIP

i don't care if she did, i'm just asking . . .

ADAM

yeah, well . . . you can be annoying.

PHILLIP

it's one of my best qualities, actually . . .

ADAM

and there aren't many of them.

PHILLIP

you really tripped? truthfully . . .

ADAM

yes.

PHILLIP

. . . huh. okay.

ADAM

why do you say that? 'huh.' you don't believe me?

PHILLIP

no, i just . . . nothing.

ADAM

what? don't do that, come on now. what?

PHILLIP

it's no big . . . (*beat.*) i saw your girlfriend the other day,
maybe, what, last thursday? you weren't in class, and
i said to her, i asked her if you were okay, that's all . . .

ADAM

yeah, so?

PHILLIP

and she said 'yes,' but you were recovering from an
operation or something . . .

ADAM

what?!

PHILLIP

that's what i said, 'he didn't tell me about anything,' and
she said it wasn't really an operation *per se*, just some
thing you had done. a procedure. and that was it . . . so
i just thought . . .

ADAM

no, it's not . . .

PHILLIP

hey, you don't have to tell me, we're not on intimate
terms or anything . . .

ADAM

i hurt it. really . . .

PHILLIP

whatever.

ADAM

no, not 'whatever.' phil . . . i did. i hit it and, you
know . . . i banged it pretty bad at home and so i had
the doctor look at it. but he didn't . . . *operate* or
anything. the bandage is from that. the door.

PHILLIP

after you tripped on the stairs . . . yeah, you told me.

ADAM

she must've just gotten confused.

PHILLIP

maybe. that doesn't seem to happen to her very often,
though . . . she's pretty sharp.

ADAM

no, she is . . . i'm sure it's just the way i explained it.
i mean, to her . . .

PHILLIP

right.

ADAM

. . . and where did you see her?

PHILLIP

evelyn? i don't know . . . starbucks or somewhere. the
mall, maybe.

ADAM

she doesn't drink coffee.

PHILLIP

so, it was downtown then, record city, i think . . . (*beat.*)
what, you worried i'm gonna steal her? believe me . . .

ADAM

no, god . . . don't be so . . . (*touches nose.*) anyway, it's
gonna be fine . . .

PHILLIP

well, that's good to hear.

ADAM

yep.

PHILLIP

. . . so you're okay, though?

ADAM

no. i mean, yeah, i'm great . . . absolutely.

PHILLIP

then good . . . (*beat.*) and you'd tell me if there was
anything seriously wrong?

ADAM

. . . of course! hey, what's up?

PHILLIP

i mean, we're friends, right? you'd come to me . . .

ADAM

. . . about what? (*beat.*) phil, what's . . .?

PHILLIP

jenny told me.

ADAM

what?

*adam looks at his friend. for the first time, phillip
seems less than in control.*

PHILLIP

she kissed you.

ADAM

oh.

PHILLIP

she felt shitty, i guess. i could tell for, like, a week that
something was going on and finally she told me about
it. how you guys met and talked about us – why do girls
always have to talk about everything? – and later she
leaned over and kissed you. that's what she told me.

ADAM

she did . . . i mean, she did do that but it was nothing.

PHILLIP

hey, it wasn't nothing, she's a good kisser. hell of a kisser.

ADAM

i don't mean 'nothing,' but it meant nothing. it didn't
hold meaning for us . . . it just happened.

PHILLIP

okay. so, you can speak for her, then?

ADAM

for me . . . it didn't for *me*. it was just a . . . that's all she said?

PHILLIP

don't tell me there's more . . .

ADAM

no, god, not at all . . . i just . . .

PHILLIP

it's alright, i'd been acting weird lately, this whole marriage idea is just . . . freaky . . . so, it's my fault.

ADAM

right . . .

PHILLIP

i mean, who gets married at *twenty-two* these days? right? it's not the middle ages, for chrissakes . . . (*beat.*) i just feel bad . . . you know, for her.

ADAM

why?

PHILLIP

kissing you . . . that's hideous! it's what those new-age dumbshits would call 'a desperate cry for help' . . .

they laugh, catching each other's eye.

ADAM

sorry . . .

PHILLIP

's alright. it's better than me having to kiss you . . .

ADAM

good point.

PHILLIP

no tongue, right?

ADAM

jesus . . .

PHILLIP

i'm just asking . . .

ADAM

no! please . . .

phillip looks at his watch.

PHILLIP

well, i got a three-ten. you?

ADAM

nah . . . i'm free. gonna go work out.

PHILLIP

you and the . . . what is going on with the 'metamorphosis'
thing here? you're like frankenstein . . .

ADAM

you mean, frankenstein's monster. frankenstein was the
doctor . . .

PHILLIP

ahh, don't be such an english lit. prick . . .

ADAM

i am an english lit. prick.

PHILLIP

i know, but you don't have to sound like one, do you? doctor, monster, whatever! what's up with that?

ADAM

nothing. it feels good.

PHILLIP

how much weight have you lost?

ADAM

not that much, maybe ten pounds or . . .

PHILLIP

.i'd say more like fifteen.

ADAM

yeah, maybe.

PHILLIP

and the hair thing going, no glasses now . . .

ADAM

it's just a few little . . .

PHILLIP

hey, it's the 'new you.' plus, the nails. jenny told me that, which is the one that i just cannot believe!

ADAM

it's a life change . . .

PHILLIP

please, don't make me throw up with the oprah-talk,
alright? i'm trying to compliment you here . . .

ADAM

. . . thanks.

PHILLIP

i used to find blood on our *phone*, okay, so it's not just
this casual thing, quitting . . .

ADAM

i know. i know that . . .

PHILLIP

alright, then. (*beat.*) no, you look good. i can see why
she kissed you . . . hell, i might even kiss you, with a few
drinks in me.

ADAM

(*laughing*) i'll run home and hide the liquor . . .

PHILLIP

please, i'll help you! (*beat.*) and nothing else happened,
right, i mean, between you and jenny?

adam stops cold. walked right into a trap.

ADAM

. . . what?

PHILLIP

i'm just asking.

ADAM

phil . . .

PHILLIP

not really looking for a speech or anything. just an
answer. she said 'no,' just so you don't think i'm laying a
trap here or whatever . . .

ADAM

i don't.

PHILLIP

. . . nobody saw you on campus or anything. a ranger
out in the woods. you know, so . . .

ADAM

. . . what's that supposed to mean?

PHILLIP

i'm just *saying*, i'll believe you, whatever you tell me. i've
got no witnesses. so . . .

ADAM

nothing happened, phil. truthfully.

PHILLIP

. . . that's not what she said.

adam freezes but doesn't falter.

ADAM

that's not true.

PHILLIP

you sure?

ADAM

yes.

PHILLIP

you're right, it's not true. hey, a man's gotta try . . .

ADAM

uh-huh . . .

PHILLIP

not that i want out of this or anything. i love scuba-
diving . . .

ADAM

of course. as we all do . . .

PHILLIP

exactly. i'm just not sure i wanna share my air tank with
the same person the rest of my life . . .

adam says nothing, just smiles.

. . . but that's my problem. (*beat.*) i gotta get to class . . .

ADAM

alright. take care.

PHILLIP

sorry for the, you know, crazy shit.

ADAM

it's okay . . .

PHILLIP

. . . don't kiss my girlfriend any more, alright?

ADAM

you got it.

PHILLIP

see you . . . we should do something again one of these
days, all of us, i mean . . .

ADAM

. . . yeah . . .

PHILLIP

if you guys wanna. let us know. so long, romeo!

ADAM

(*pulling on a coat*) knock it off!

*phillip starts off but stops dead. he turns back and
studies adam.*

PHILLIP

. . . where's your jacket?

ADAM

what?

PHILLIP

okay, this is too much. the cord jacket, the lumberjacky-
looking thing . . .

ADAM

i dunno . . .

PHILLIP

and this, umm, tommy hilfiger-ish job, where'd you come
up with that?

ADAM

. . . the mall. i bought it.

PHILLIP

you bought some clothes? you, like, went out to the mall
on your bike and actually . . .

ADAM

no, evelyn drove me. so? what's the big . . .?

PHILLIP

the deal is this . . . you've had that frumpy-looking
fucker for three years, probably more, and i've never
seen you out of it. *ever.* winter, the dead of summer,
whatever, you've got that coat on. and now you're just
like, 'hey, whatever, (*yawns*) yeah, i bought the ol' stars
and stripes here with evelyn.' that's like a sailing slicker!

ADAM

it's their yachtsman line . . .

PHILLIP

i am gonna puke here, i swear to god! i did not just hear
you use the word 'yachtsman' . . .

ADAM

hey, she likes it . . .

PHILLIP

well, isn't that just neat? and peachy keen and whatever
other *little house on the prairie* shit you wanna spout . . .
what i wanna know is, do you like it?

ADAM

. . . it's okay.

PHILLIP

not what i said. i asked, 'do-you-like-it?'

ADAM

it's fine. it's a coat . . .

PHILLIP

and lemme ask you . . . did you keep the cord job or did she make you toss it?

ADAM

. . . who cares? this is . . . i threw it out, okay? goodwill, actually.

PHILLIP

'goodwill, actually.'

ADAM

it's really no big deal . . .

PHILLIP

dude, don't just say 'no big deal.' i begged you to throw out the farm coat our freshman year, i mean, you've lost *both* of us a lot of dates with that thing on! you've had it since, like, birth, okay, so do me a little favour and let's not pretend that the jacket and the, ahh, weight and the jon bon jovi hair are no big deal. because when it comes to routine, you used to be like mister goddamn *rogers*!

ADAM

phil, it's a fucking jacket so just lay off. go to class . . .

PHILLIP

uh-huh. fine . . .

ADAM

fine.

i just hope next time we pass each other i recognize who
the hell you are . . .

ADAM

well, if not, you and evelyn can always head over to
record city and have a chat . . .

PHILLIP

hey, i wouldn't get too deep into the moral issues during
this particular conversation . . . okay, romeo? i may have
a big fucking mouth, but at least i keep it to myself . . .

*they stare at each other, a nearly visible wall going up
between them. adam blinks first and walks off. phillip
watches him go.*

so long, matey!

evelyn stands with jenny at a high table, sipping hot drinks.

EVELYN

. . . and you, everything's good?

JENNY

yeah, you know. okay.

EVELYN

huh. well, that's nice to hear . . .

JENNY

you?

EVELYN

oh, you know, pretty great. just studying, working on my art . . .

JENNY

right, you've got a big thing you're doing, or, what do you call it?

EVELYN

thesis project. for my degree . . .

JENNY

that's terrific.

EVELYN

yeah. the showing's in a couple weeks . . .

JENNY

and it's going well? what is it again?

EVELYN

i never said . . .

JENNY

oh, well, that's why.

EVELYN

right. (*beat.*) it's this sculpture thingie . . .

JENNY

nice. mmmm, i love the arts.

EVELYN

really?

JENNY

yeah, you know, going to movies and stuff. we don't get
so many here, we have to drive into the city for any of
the newer releases, but i see a lot of videos. phil watches
'em constantly.

EVELYN

yeah, and what kind does he like?

JENNY

oh, a bunch, but more artsy ones than i do . . . *aliens.*
blade runner. twelve monkeys. is that right, or were there
ten of 'em?

EVELYN

no, it was twelve . . . a dozen monkeys, i think, all
together.

JENNY

anyway, that kind. sci-fi, but with some meaning, too.
and action.

EVELYN

huh. that's great . . . i hate sci-fi. (*beat.*) and you? what
kind do you like, jenny?

JENNY

ummm, any, i don't mind . . . but i usually like at least
some romance in them. that's always nice.

   evelyn studies her for a moment.

EVELYN

yes . . . romance's good. especially when you least expect
it.

JENNY

uh-huh . . .

   *jenny looks over, sees that evelyn is watching her,
   looks away quickly.*

. . . you know, i was gonna say, i think what you've done
with adam, it's really great.

EVELYN

and what've i done?

JENNY

you know, just . . . he's changed.

EVELYN

that's right. *he's* changed.

JENNY

that's what i mean.

EVELYN

he's done the work . . .

JENNY

of course, i didn't mean that you . . .

EVELYN

i know. i'm just saying, he did it.

JENNY

right. that's always what they say, though, isn't it?

EVELYN

what? and who are they?

JENNY

you know, like, in *cosmo*, when they have those tests,
asking what you'd like to change about your guy . . .

EVELYN

ahhh. now you're gonna get all scientific on me . . .

JENNY

it's true, though, right? almost everybody i've gone
out with, if you could alter just one thing, or even get
them to stop wearing sunglasses up on their head all
the time . . . then they'd be perfect. it's that sort of deal,
isn't it?

EVELYN

something like that . . . or it could just be that i care
about him.

JENNY

phil's got, like, six of those 'one things,' but it's the same
idea . . .

EVELYN

right. and how is ol' phil?

JENNY

he's . . . phil. six 'things' away from being amazing . . .

*adam arrives at the table, obviously unprepared to
find both women waiting for him. he wears no
bandage.*

ADAM

. . . hey, evelyn. hi. jenny, hello.

EVELYN/JENNY

hi, adam. hello.

ADAM

i didn't know you guys were . . .

EVELYN

i invited her.

ADAM

that's alright, then . . .

JENNY

i like your new jacket! phil told me about it . . .

ADAM

oh, right. yeah. it's . . . new.

JENNY

and your nose! god, you okay?

ADAM

yep. 'course . . . it was nothing.

JENNY

falling down's not nothing. (*studies him.*) looks okay,
though . . .

*an uncomfortable pause. evelyn looks over at adam,
who clears his throat.*

EVELYN

you *fell?*

ADAM

. . . yeah. anyway . . .

EVELYN

anyway, pull up some floor . . . we got you a cocoa.

he moves warily to them, squeezing in next to evelyn.

ADAM

thanks. (*to evelyn*) you don't drink coffee . . .

EVELYN

it's not. it's decaf . . .

ADAM

that's still coffee.

EVELYN

good point. so i drink coffee, then, i just don't like the
caffeine . . .

JENNY

me either.

EVELYN

really? you don't like caffeine, either, jenny? did you
know that, too, adam, that jenny doesn't like caffeine?

ADAM

no. i didn't know that . . .

EVELYN

see? there's lots you don't know . . .

they all sip their drinks silently for a moment.

jenny was just saying that she thinks you're great . . .
i mean, doing great things with yourself.

ADAM

yeah? thanks, jenny . . .

JENNY

you're welcome. i just . . .

EVELYN

she thinks you're just about perfect now, don't you, jen?

JENNY

i didn't say that.

EVELYN

so, he's not perfect, then? obviously his motor control's
a bit off, if he fell, but . . .

JENNY

i said that you guys are . . .

ADAM

forget about it.

EVELYN

it's true, i'm exaggerating. she said, and i paraphrase,
'he's changed.' but she implied for the better . . .

ADAM

well, i agree. i have. and again, thank you.

JENNY

welcome . . .

EVELYN

i think you've changed, too, adam. a lot.

ADAM

yeah? how's that?

EVELYN

well, i mean, it's obvious, all the minor things are pretty
obvious, but in subtler ways as well . . . you've gotten
cuter. and stronger. more confident. and craftier . . .

ADAM

'craftier,' huh?

EVELYN

apparently so . . . that spill you took must've done it.

JENNY

i'm sorry, am i missing something?

ADAM

i'm not sure . . . (*to evelyn*) evelyn, what's up?

EVELYN

nothing. not a thing . . .

JENNY

i mean, you knew about him hurting himself, didn't you?
(*to adam*) phil said you had a big bandage on, so i just
figured . . .

EVELYN

no, jenny, i saw it. i'm kidding . . .

JENNY

ahh. i couldn't tell . . .

EVELYN

sometimes it's hard to read me. know when i'm joking . . .

ADAM

very hard.

EVELYN

it is. but i am . . . joking, i mean. adam took a bad fall
and smashed his nose, but he's okay now . . . see?

*she grabs adam's face and holds it out for jenny to
look. adam pulls away, a bit too quickly.*

. . . it healed well, don't you think?

JENNY

yes.

ADAM

do you guys wanna salad or something? i'm hungry . . .

EVELYN

i'm fine. jenny . . . hungry?

JENNY

i'm okay. (*to adam*) your nose looks . . . how much
weight have you lost?

ADAM

not that much, really.

EVELYN

twenty-one pounds. (*to adam*) i peeked, is that alright?

he glares at her; jenny tries to keep up.

JENNY

'peeked?'

EVELYN

his journal . . . a record of his progress that he's keeping.
twenty-one pounds as of . . .

ADAM

. . . last friday. yeah.

JENNY

really? that's so cool . . .

EVELYN

cosmo story in the making, huh?

JENNY

yep.

ADAM

it's good, yeah, i've been keeping at it . . .

EVELYN

she knows, adam, she already said you've 'changed.' and
i already agreed. we're past that . . .

ADAM

okay, i'm, like, totally lost here . . .

EVELYN

you're mentioned in there, too, jenny.

JENNY

where?

EVELYN

adam's journal. i mean, it's a veiled entry but i think it's
you . . .

ADAM

evelyn . . .

EVELYN

i peeked twice. (*to jenny*) you're right next to someone
known as 'cute waitress.'

JENNY

(*cautiously*) . . . why's that? i mean . . . adam?

ADAM

you're not. it's . . . she's . . .

EVELYN

something about a meeting . . . and a drive after, in your
cute little v-dub . . .

ADAM

what're you saying?! jenny, there's not any . . .

jenny picks up her purse and smiles thinly.

JENNY

you know what? it's pretty late, i should get . . .

ADAM

no, don't go . . . (*to evelyn*) why are you doing this?

EVELYN

i'm just having coffee. decaf.

JENNY

i need to go.

EVELYN

i just wanna talk about the kiss. why can't we do that?

the moment hangs. jenny stops short.

we should just put it out there . . . i'm very open, and
i just feel that . . .

ADAM

this is inappropriate, okay?

JENNY

(*to adam*) did you tell her about the . . .?

EVELYN

no, no, he didn't . . . phillip did. days ago. we met and
he told me all about it, jenny. what you told him,
anyway. the rest i got from loverboy's diary . . .

JENNY

. . . adam?

ADAM

she's making that up . . . she's . . .

EVELYN

am i?

ADAM

yes!

EVELYN

then set the record straight . . .

ADAM

i don't wanna do this right now.

EVELYN

seems a touch late for that.

JENNY

(*to evelyn*) phillip told you about our talk? when? (*beat.*)
what else did he tell you?

EVELYN

lots of things . . . he's a very chatty guy, when you wind
him up.

JENNY

. . . i can't believe it . . .

EVELYN

then you're never gonna believe the rest of this . . .

ADAM

evelyn, let's just drop it, okay? if you're angry with me,
alright, but this is not . . .

EVELYN

we're just talking. people need to share more, that's how
this stuff happens, this covert stuff, because we hide it . . .

JENNY

fine . . . you want to . . . go ahead. adam wrote something
in his journal, obviously, and i told phil about . . .

ADAM

jenny, i didn't . . .

JENNY

what do you wanna hear? we kissed.

EVELYN

no, i knew that . . . i'm sorry, i've confused you. i meant
about my kiss. with phillip. that's the part i wanted to
talk about with you guys . . . i didn't make that clear?

JENNY

. . . what?

ADAM

that's bullshit . . .

EVELYN

no, that's getting even. (*beat.*) unless you guys have
something else to tell me about. meaning, 'the drive' . . .

ADAM

we didn't go on any . . .

JENNY

that's not true. you didn't meet phil . . .

EVELYN

ask him.

JENNY

. . . or he would've told me . . . he . . .

EVELYN

apparently not.

JENNY

. . . i'm going. i'm going now, 'kay?

EVELYN

fine, then we'll just let that one hang for a bit . . . the
woods, i mean.

JENNY

i'll . . . see you. adam, i'm . . .

EVELYN

(*calling to her*) you guys are still coming to my showing,
right? phillip said you would!

*she is gone. adam takes a careful sip before speaking.
he turns to evelyn, about to speak, when jenny returns.*

JENNY

(*directly at evelyn*) hey . . . look, i don't know why i'm
here, i guess i came back to say 'i'm sorry.' sorry if i've
offended you in some way, or done something to make
you so indifferent to me, cold or whatever. and i don't
mean what's happened, i don't, because i think you've
been this way the whole time i've known you. so . . . sorry
i'm not an artsy person or cool enough or, you know, i'm
not super-smart, sorry about that. but as far as just *being*
a person, like, an average-type person . . . i'm pretty
okay. i am. (*beat.*) that kinda came out bad, i mean,
dumb, so i'm just gonna . . . yeah. (*she wanders off.*)

ADAM

. . . okay, that was horrible.

EVELYN

oh, i dunno . . . i could've told her about the blow job
i gave him. (*beat.*) kidding . . .

ADAM

no, listen, what you did was shitty, and awful and just
plain wrong . . .

EVELYN

as opposed to you two sneaking off and making out?
where would that fall on the 'bad behaviour' list . . . ?

ADAM

you had no right to do that.

EVELYN

true.

ADAM

make her feel that way . . .

EVELYN

she's got a boyfriend who's shit. now she knows. hell,
she already knew . . .

ADAM

it was still wrong to treat her like that! and me.

EVELYN

yeah, let's talk about you . . .

ADAM

go ahead. you seem raring to go.

EVELYN

you wanna tell me about the rest of your date, or should
i . . . ?

ADAM

she called me, okay, asked if i could get together and
talk, you know, about phil. and them.

EVELYN

and then you made out. most natural thing in the
world . . .

ADAM

it just happened. look, i was going to say something . . .

EVELYN

that was hitler's excuse. try another one . . .

ADAM

it was a mistake! okay? i know that . . .

EVELYN

and how *big* was that mistake? (*beat.*) i don't care about
what happened. i don't. i just want the truth . . . i told
you about what i did – you think i wanted to kiss that
guy? – i only did it for the effect. but i'm asking you . . .
what else went on? i deserve to know.

ADAM

. . . nothing.

EVELYN

you're sticking with that?

ADAM

yes.

EVELYN

even if i tell you i know something else went on.

ADAM

how could you? it didn't . . . and i did not put any
'drive' in my journal. that was a lie.

EVELYN

no, it was a *bluff*. because i could sense it . . . (*beat*.) and
the waitress *was* there . . .

ADAM

i'm telling you the truth. about jenny, i mean . . .

EVELYN

i don't believe you.

ADAM

. . . i am!

EVELYN

then we'll have to leave it at that. won't we?

  they stare at one another. she touches her nose.

oh, and glad to hear about your trip . . . see you next
fall.

ADAM

that's a bad joke . . .

EVELYN

it's a worse lie . . .

ADAM

what was i gonna tell them? huh?

EVELYN

the truth?

ADAM

come on . . . i took shit about my new jacket! that's all
people say to me any more, 'what's up with you? what's

going on?' i can't exactly spread it around about what
i've done . . .

EVELYN

what? you *fell* . . .

ADAM

what're we doing here?

EVELYN

i dunno. you tell me . . .

ADAM

i don't know. i really don't . . .

EVELYN

are you tired of me? 's that it?

ADAM

god, no! are you nuts?!

EVELYN

then i don't get it . . . i don't wanna sound ol'-fashioned
here, but you're a step away from fucking around on
me . . .

ADAM

i would never do that . . .

EVELYN

no, you would never do that with *her*, and mostly because
she wouldn't. i know the type, she needed a shoulder,
well, what the hell, why not a kiss while she's at it, and
maybe a quick hand job. who knows? but she's not gonna
screw you and you probably wouldn't be able to get it
up, anyway, because he's your best 'bud.' (*beat*.) but

lemme ask you, adam, if it hadn't been her, if it'd been, oh, say that 'cute waitress' the other night . . .

adam looks away; evelyn doesn't let up.

. . . didn't think i caught that, did you? the chatty-chat and the extra three bucks on the tip.

ADAM
. . . that was nothing.

EVELYN
it's never anything. until it's something . . . (*beat.*) if it'd been her instead . . . out on that drive . . .

ADAM
. . . we-didn't-go-for-a . . .

EVELYN
. . . whatever. but if she'd been there instead, then what? just ask yourself.

ADAM
jesus, next you're gonna tell me the handkerchief with the strawberries on it is missing . . .

EVELYN
i don't know that reference.

ADAM
don't worry about it. (*pleads.*) evelyn, please . . .

she smiles and begins more gently.

EVELYN
i just wanna know where we stand . . . i thought i could trust you.

ADAM

you can!

EVELYN

she's your friend's fiancée, adam. i'm your girlfriend . . .
where's the trust in that?

he takes her hand suddenly.

ADAM

i'll do anything you want. okay? i know what i did was
wrong, i do, i messed up but i've never done that before.
lied to a person i was going out with . . . shit, i haven't
even gone out with someone for the two years before we
met! so, tell me what to do and i'll do it . . . i just, i just
don't wanna lose you.

EVELYN

you're sure . . .?

ADAM

i am so sure. i love you . . .

EVELYN

i told you, that's a big word . . .

ADAM

. . . and i'm using it. i do, completely.

EVELYN

anything i say?

ADAM

anything.

EVELYN

(*without emotion*) give them up. as friends, both of
them. no explanation. don't see them or speak to them
again. not ever.

ADAM

. . . huh?

EVELYN

that's what i want. that's the proof to me about how
you feel . . .

ADAM

evelyn . . . that's . . .

EVELYN

one should always be careful when asking to be put to
a test . . .

ADAM

. . . jesus christ . . .

EVELYN

so, what's it gonna be, adam?

ADAM

and if i don't . . . ?

EVELYN

pretty much like these things end. i mean, in life, at least
. . . if this was a movie, i'd see the light eventually, but
no such luck. final answer?

   adam stares at her for a long moment.

ADAM

. . . i choose you.

she pulls him close and kisses him for a long time.

EVELYN

you choose well, grasshopper . . .

AN AUDITORIUM

phillip standing around, dressed up. adam enters,
holding a glass of punch, tries to go the other way but
phil stops him.

PHILLIP
. . . adam, dude, what's up?!

ADAM
(*looking around*) hey, phil. how's it going?

PHILLIP
you know, okay. so, what, you don't take my calls now?

ADAM
no, i've been . . . i mean . . .

PHILLIP
's okay, i understand. the whole . . . thing . . .

ADAM
nah, it's just been busy lately. at work and stuff . . .

PHILLIP
yeah. whatever.

ADAM
seriously. (*beat.*) i need to get a seat . . .

PHILLIP
hold on, hey . . . where's the fire?

ADAM
(*nervously*) i just wanna . . . good spot. (*beat.*) where's
jenny?

PHILLIP

funny.

ADAM

what?

PHILLIP

man, come on . . . we broke up. broke it off, whatever.
you knew that.

ADAM

what? no, i, when . . . ?

PHILLIP

like, two weeks ago . . . right after . . . you know. and
i'm sorry about that. i was pissed off, but, i mean . . . no
call for that 'eye for an eye' shit.

ADAM

. . . it's okay. but you and jenny're . . . ? i can't believe that.

PHILLIP

believe it. (*beat*.) she came over one day, after seeing you
guys, i guess, and that was it. the ring off, and gone.

ADAM

. . . i'm sorry.

PHILLIP

listen, no hard feelings . . . i was looking to get out, you
know that. but once you start making those plans, you
know, like picking out *napkins* and shit, it's almost easier
to just do the thing! (*beat*.) you did me a favour, really . . .
too young to get hitched.

ADAM

i don't know what to say . . .

PHILLIP

don't worry about it. (*beat.*) you haven't seen her lately, have you? jenny, i mean . . .

ADAM

no . . .

PHILLIP

'kay. anyway, this oughta be good, huh?!

they share a light laugh. jenny walks up the aisle, sees them and goes for a seat.

ADAM

jenny, hi . . .

JENNY

oh, adam . . . hello. hi, phil.

PHILLIP

hey.

ADAM

i'm sorry about . . . you guys . . .

JENNY

(*glaring at phil*) boy, you just can't keep anything to yourself, can you?

PHILLIP

what?

JENNY

you never change . . . that's what. (*she turns and walks off, taking a place in the auditorium.*)

ADAM

what's she . . . ?

PHILLIP

it's not, like, totally *official* yet . . . ahh, fuck, what're
you gonna do?

the lights flicker twice. adam looks up.

ADAM

we should find a place to . . .

PHILLIP

(*looking*) there's two over there.

ADAM

umm . . . maybe we shouldn't . . .

PHILLIP

. . . got it. okay, whatever. take care, man.

*he wanders off. adam watches him go, then finds a
place to sit.*

*lights go down, theatrical lights up. after a moment,
evelyn (dressed up for her) enters crisply and smiles.*

EVELYN

good evening. thank you for coming out tonight – it's
very cold and rainy and i'm sure this is not how most
of you would choose to spend your time away from
campus . . . *on* campus. so, i promise to make this
presentation as quick and painless as possible, for some
of you at least, and get you back home as swiftly as
i can. the accompanying visual portion of this graduate
thesis project is currently under review but will hopefully

be available in the exhibition gallery down the hall for
your perusal next week, so if you don't stay tonight
for punch and cookies, umm, please stop by and take
a look at your convenience. (*smiles.*) okay, that's the
boring stuff . . .

  she turns over a note card.

my task here tonight is to unveil my semester's work,
explain it and then smile and shake hands, leaving a few
of you to examine it, grade it, etc. in essence, be at your
mercy. which is fine, since i realize i have been my entire
academic life – at someone's mercy, that is – which reaches
back to when i was five. so be it . . . that's the system
and one person can't change it . . . but perhaps they can
make you question that system and your values just a
little bit. thus, my rather, ahh, dramatic presentation at
this time. (*looks over card.*) blah-blah-blah . . .

  *evelyn starts to move but steps back into the light, as
  if she's forgotten something.*

oh, i almost forgot . . . and this is fairly personal,
probably shouldn't even do it but it really is the capper
to my time here at clarkson, so please indulge me. (*beat.*)
i was given an engagement ring two days ago and
i haven't answered the guy yet . . . so i wanted to do it
this evening. here goes. this is a beautiful stone and an
amazing gesture on your part, for many reasons. by the
time i'm through here, i promise that you'll have your
answer . . .

  she shows the ring off to the audience.

my graduate advisor gave me this advice five months
ago . . . 'strive to make art, but change the world.' pretty

wise words, i thought, at the time, and so, being a good
little student, that's what i set out to do. as you know,
every journey begins with a single step – boy, the 'coffee
cup slogans' are coming hard and fast tonight – and so
i set out to . . .

> *she appears almost nervous, but not quite. she looks
> at the audience for a moment.*

as i looked around my world for something to change,
i knew i'd been given a tall order. 'change the world.' so,
i decided to do the next best thing, which was change
someone's world. i mean, that's a start, right? one person
changes, and then another, and then, well, you get it . . .
crude but effective. with that in mind, i present to you
this, my newest work. it is a *human* sculpture on which
i've worked these past eighteen weeks, and of whom
i'm very proud. i cannot legally name him tonight as
he hasn't yet signed a waiver for the various items on
display in the visual portion, but it's a small college, and
a smaller town (*laughs*), so you've got a pretty decent
chance at guessing who it is. in fact, i've done all i could
to be as visible as possible with him this year – i'm more
of a stay-at-home person myself – since i thought that
was an important aspect of his unique transformation.
the piece itself – him – is untitled since i think, i hope,
that it will mean something different to each of you and,
frankly, anyone who sees it. His own name, however, is
quite apropos.

> *she turns over a large photograph from a nearby easel.
> the face has been blurred out.*

i did the mtv thing here on the face . . . this is a 'before'
picture that i had a classmate take of us near the pizza
hut out by the highway. that was our first official

encounter after he asked me out – at his place of work, a big no-no, or so i was told – and it was here that i coaxed him into eating his first vegetarian meal. well, as vegetarian as a spinach-and-mushroom calzone can be! he also had a salad . . . anyway, he told me that for him, it was a huge deal and it does mark the beginning of my systematic makeover, or 'sculpting,' if you will, of my two very pliable materials of choice: the human flesh and the human will. (*beat.*) i first spotted my chosen base material . . . it's so funny not to use names! sorry, but a lawyer actually told me i had to say that, 'base material' . . . on january 9th, the fifth day of winter semester, as i was actively pursuing another set of 'base material.' (*grins.*) obviously, my current creation appeared much more right for my work and so i created a scenario that would allow for our eventual, yet seemingly random, connection.

she scans the audience.

still with me? you're very quiet . . . okay. the exhibit itself will give you many first-hand examples of my efforts, some hands-on such as video tapes or sound recordings of our conversations and others more scientific in nature, as in growth charts, x-rays and accompanying data. as you can see from this photo, however, the hair, the glasses, the excessive amount of weight, offered a number of physical areas that made him unique and perfect for this project. a short list of alterations i've induced would include eating better and losing weight – some twenty-five pounds or more – an exercise regimen that included both cardiovascular work and weight training, the purchase of contact lenses, a complete change in hairstyles and significant wardrobe alterations as well. he even tattooed his body for me, without asking . . . in a highly questionable place. these are surface items, to be sure, but if i, in fact, tell you that i'm going through with it and marrying the guy, you'd probably all shake my hand and say, 'wow, how the hell can i do that to my boyfriend?' but this, i'm afraid, was not done out of love or caring or concern . . . this was a simple matter of can i instil 'x' amount of change in this creature, using only manipulation as my palette knife? i made sure that nothing was ever forced during our sessions or 'sittings' together – i can't really say they were dates, not on my part, although the allusion of 'dating' was imperative – and that his free will was always at the forefront of each decision. i coaxed, made suggestions, created the illusion of interest and desire, but never said, 'please do this.' not once. any questions yet?

she scans the crowd.

ummmm . . . you may be asking yourselves, 'well, did she at least tell him?' of course not, no, i couldn't. not until tonight, or he really wouldn't be a piece of art. he would be a jilted lover, a spurned fiancé, etc. but he is more than that . . . he's my creation. now, it'll be easy for many of you to condemn my actions as harsh, inhumane or unrealistic as you drive or walk home tonight, but remember this, like so many of you when pursuing your personal best in relationships and at work . . . i was interested in humanity, yes, but insistent on results above all else. how many here can say that they have never looked at their significant other and/or a business associate and said, 'they're perfect, they're great, except for just *one* thing . . .' well, i too have taken my base materials and honed them into something new, something unique and, in the eyes and standards of society, something arguably improved. but, with the artist's ruthless pursuit of truth and historical disregard for rule and law . . . i've gone a step further. i found

that, with the right coaxing of my material – yes,
'coaxing' often of a sexual nature, i'll admit – i could
hone the inside of my sculpture as well as the surface.
i found myself suddenly creating strong moral ambiguity
where i could detect only the slightest traces before,
often in direct proportion to the amount of external
change. this means, as my subject became handsomer
and firmer and more confident, his actions became more
and more, ahh, *questionable*. against medical advice,
he had work done to his face, cosmetic surgery at age
twenty-two, and insisted to those around him that he
had merely fallen down. he also started to deceive his
friends and myself with greater abandon during this
period while showing increased interest in other women.
indeed, he had relations with his best friend's fiancée and
continues to harbour details from us about the incident
to this day. moreover, he was willing to give those
friends up when asked, walk away from them without
any further contact, after said encounter, leading me to
an assumption of further wrong-doing with the young
woman in question. and, as stated earlier, these universal
corrections culminated in an offer of marriage to me,
this coming from a confirmed, albeit young, bachelor.
i call this act 'morally questionable' because it seems to
be motivated, in my mind at least, as much out of guilt
as genuine feelings for me. he has then, as i see it, been
utterly and totally refashioned as a person. (*beat*.) as my
grandfather used to say, 'he's a real piece of work . . .'

   she holds up a large 'after' photo for all to see.

and yet open any fashion magazine, turn on any television
programme and the world will tell you . . . he's only
gotten more interesting, more desirable, more normal. in
a word, *better*. he is a living, breathing example of our
obsession with the surface of things, the shape of them.

121

(*beat.*) now, my work will fade, to be sure. like chipping marble or crazing paint, it will succumb to a can of pringles, a late morning in bed. to time itself. but for this one glorious moment, it is perfect. as perfect as i made it . . . (*to photo*) not bad, huh? and ladies, he is available. (*to adam*) this was a startling and unexpected gesture, but obviously, i can't accept . . .

she takes off the ring and places it on an easel.

you can examine the stone and setting further when it's placed in the exhibit. (*beat.*) as for me, i have no regrets or feelings of remorse for my actions, the manufactured emotions . . . none of it. i have always stood by the single and simple conceit that i am an artist. only that. i follow in a long tradition of artists who believe that there is no such concept as religion, or government, community or even family. there is only art. art that must be created. whatever the cost. (*beat.*) with that in mind, i present you with my untitled sculpture and supporting materials tonight. thank you.

she takes a short bow and steps out of the light.

several podiums scattered about with various 'supporting data' on them.

evelyn standing all alone, punch in one hand, cookie in the other. after a moment, she takes a nibble. she crosses to a box of photos and browses. adam enters and stares at her.

ADAM

. . . not a big 'modern art' crowd, i guess, huh?

EVELYN

hey. (*beat.*) glad you stopped by . . .

ADAM

yeah, well, i didn't really have anything to do . . . plus, i can't show my face in the streets, so it seemed logical.

EVELYN

look, adam . . .

ADAM

please don't 'look, adam' me now, okay, or i might not make it through this . . . (*beat.*) just refer to me as 'it' or 'untitled,' it'll help me keep some perspective here . . .

he wanders over and pours some punch. stuffs a few cookies in his pocket. shoves three in his mouth and chews them down.

. . . that's gonna shoot some piece of data all to shit, isn't it?

EVELYN

doesn't matter now, do what you want . . . you're
finished.

ADAM

'you're finished.' wow. (*considers.*) most people just say,
'hey, sorry, can't marry you.' and they say it in private . . .

EVELYN

. . . yeah, that might've been a bit too far.

ADAM

oh shit, evelyn, you are so beyond 'far' that you're in
danger of hitting uranus. and i mean the planet . . .

EVELYN

(*smiling*) see, you're still funny . . .

ADAM

just stop, alright? i was never funny, ever, or good-looking
or clever. i was nothing until you started dicking around
with me. i admit it. no-thing. but you know what? i was
absolutely fine with that . . .

EVELYN

i know this is a lot for you to take in and everything . . .

ADAM

uh-huh . . . i got a little gregor samsa thing going right
now, so . . .

EVELYN

i don't get that . . .

ADAM

doesn't matter. i do . . . i get it.

a moment of dead silence.

EVELYN

. . . listen, i know my work relied on not telling you
what was going on, but i . . .

ADAM

here in a 'small town' we just call it lying . . .

EVELYN

i did lie to you, yes . . .

ADAM

yeah, just a little. (*beat.*) 'i'm a very straightforward
person . . .'

EVELYN

i had to say that. sorry.

ADAM

you're sorry? well, that's good . . . i figured i was gonna
have to really work to get that one out of you.

EVELYN

i'm not sorry. i mean, not for what i've done. i just feel
bad that you're so upset . . .

ADAM

oh, i see . . .

EVELYN

i even thought maybe you could handle it. i did, really . . .
otherwise i wouldn't have invited you tonight.

ADAM

yeah, just me and two hundred of my closest friends.

EVELYN

adam, you don't have any friends. (*beat.*) you gave up
the only ones i've known you to have. gave 'em up
pretty easily . . .

*adam shivers at this one; she's turned out to be a cool
little number.*

ADAM

geez . . . don't hold back at all, please. call it exactly
how you see it.

EVELYN

i just want to keep it as truthful as possible.

ADAM

(*laughing*) that'll be different . . .

EVELYN

. . . you're *so* angry . . .

ADAM

well, you know, evelyn, what do you want me to say?!
you messed with my life and you put it under fucking
glass . . . that might make anyone a touch cross.

EVELYN

what'd i do wrong? (*beat.*) seriously, tell me . . .

ADAM

screw you . . .

EVELYN

you have screwed me. a lot. you wanna watch it? there's
a cassette over there somewhere.

ADAM

you are seriously twisted up. i mean it . . .

EVELYN

yeah . . . what was so bad? i wanna know, tell me . . .
from your perspective.

ADAM

i'm not gonna give you a last little thrill. fuck that.

EVELYN

listen to your mouth, adam . . . you never used to talk
like that.

ADAM

you're gonna take credit for that, too, huh?

EVELYN

nope, you picked that up all on your own. cute guys
always have potty mouths. they think it makes 'em
cuter . . .

ADAM

yeah, well, tell me how 'cute' this one is, then . . . up
yours, you heartless cunt.

EVELYN

so, tell me then. go ahead, you feel that way about me,
you can tell me what i did wrong. *if* i did something
wrong . . .

ADAM

you don't see this as wrong?!

EVELYN

i said, you tell me. i wanna know what you think i did . . .

he stops for a moment, taking a deep breath. not really wanting to engage.

ADAM

you honestly have no concept here . . .

EVELYN

just say it . . .

ADAM

awww, shit. look . . . i don't have time, okay? i'm not gonna stand here and . . .

EVELYN

the exercising? or was it the new clothes that really bugged you?

ADAM

that is not the . . .

EVELYN

everything i did made you a more desirable person, adam. people began to notice you . . . take interest in you. i watched them . . .

ADAM

well, lucky me. i got to be part of your installation 'thingie.'

EVELYN

you are my installation thingie . . . (*beat.*) look, if you hadn't been here tonight, hadn't heard all this stuff . . . wouldn't you still be happy? waiting at home for me, hoping this went well, wanting to make love . . .

ADAM

that's not the point . . .

EVELYN

yes, it is! it's the *total* point. all that stuff we did was real
for you, therefore it was real. it wasn't for me, therefore
it wasn't. it's all subjective, adam. everything.

ADAM

not love. not cruelty.

EVELYN

of course they are . . .

ADAM

(reaching) i'll tell you something 'real,' i should sue your
ass.

EVELYN

you could . . . i did take that risk.

ADAM

that's right, you did, and you're crazy if you think i'm
gonna let you put all this shit on display. our time
together. *(points.)* those're our video tapes, aren't they?
the . . . sex ones. they are! you are nuts . . .

EVELYN

there's a lot of stuff here. i haven't even put it all out
yet . . .

ADAM

well, you might as well keep it packed up, then.

EVELYN

you should be proud of it . . . most of it . . .

ADAM

just save it, 'kay?

EVELYN

well, what about your jacket? where should i put that?

ADAM

. . . what?

EVELYN

your old jacket. the one i sprayed my number in, at
the museum. (*beat.*) it was only four bucks at the
goodwill . . .

ADAM

. . . why would you buy that?

EVELYN

just so i'd have it. in case . . .

ADAM

so, blackmail, too, huh? ohh, shit . . . (*beat.*) which page
of the 'scorned girls' handbook' is that on?

EVELYN

i dunno, but i bet it's in there . . .

ADAM

i do not doubt it.

EVELYN

just wanted you to know, that's all . . .

*he scans the room, then throws his hands up. he
wanders about.*

ADAM

. . . fine.

EVELYN

what?

ADAM

it's fine, forget it . . .

EVELYN

what is?

ADAM

what the hell . . . it can't get any worse. you get off
on showing people my old socks and scuzzy sheets, go
for it . . .

EVELYN

i don't 'get off' on it . . .

ADAM

it means so much to you, have a field day . . .

EVELYN

. . . adam, this is my work. (*beat.*) i'll give back whatever
you want, soon as i get my grade.

ADAM

whatever . . .

EVELYN

i will.

ADAM

the ring'd be nice. it was my grandma's.

EVELYN

i'll take care of it.

ADAM

thanks. good . . .

EVELYN

(*honestly*) . . . hard feelings?

ADAM

me? nah . . . we had some fun, right?

EVELYN

yeah.

ADAM

but, hey, that's subjective.

EVELYN

exactly.

ADAM

then *i* had some fun, fell in love and all that . . . and you got yourself a grade and a column inch or two in the college paper. congrats. seriously . . . but do me a favour, don't fool yourself and think that this is 'art.' 'kay? it's a sick fucking joke, but it is not 'art.'

EVELYN

is that right?

ADAM

pretty much, yeah. (*beat.*) you know, when picasso took a shit, he didn't call it a 'sculpture.' he knew the difference. that's what made him picasso. and if i'm wrong about that, i mean, if i totally miss the point here and somehow puking up your own little shitty neuroses all over people's laps *is* actually art, then you oughta at least realize there's a price to it all . . . you know? somebody pays for your two minutes on cnn. someone always pays for people like you. and if you don't get that, if you can't see at least *that* much . . . then you're about two inches away from using babies to make lamp shapes and calling it 'furniture.' (*beat.*) look, i know they call it the 'art scene,' but that's not all it should make. a scene. it should be more than that. anybody can be provocative, or shocking. stand up in class, or at the mall, wherever, and take a piss, paint yourself blue and run naked through a church screaming out the names of people you've slept with. is that art, or did you just forget to take your ritalin? there's gotta be a line. for art to exist, there has to be a line out there somewhere. a line between really saying something and just . . . needing attention. (*beat*) . . . i guess i'm done.

EVELYN

wow. okay . . . so, you're saying i should be a 'better person.' is that it?

ADAM

that's the nutshell, yeah.

EVELYN

better like . . . you?

ADAM

no. just better . . .

EVELYN

well, we'll just have to agree to disagree, then, won't we?

ADAM

yes, we will. we will definitely do that. (*beat.*) don't forget what oscar wilde said . . .

EVELYN

he always had something to say, didn't he?

ADAM

yeah . . . 'all art is quite useless.' he said that.

EVELYN

huh. i thought you were gonna go with 'insincerity and treachery somehow seem inseparable from the artistic temperment.' that's a good one, too . . .

ADAM

it is, yeah. damn, wish i'd said that.

EVELYN

don't worry about it . . . look how he ended up.

ADAM

yep . . . alone, penniless and in prison. everything i wish for you . . . (*he smiles.*) tell me, though. one thing.

EVELYN

yes?

ADAM

was any of it true?

EVELYN

what do you mean?

ADAM

not the things we did, or the kind words or whatever . . . but any of it?

EVELYN

. . . no. not really.

ADAM

i mean about you. the nose-job or lake forest or your
mother's maiden name? one thing you ever said to me?

EVELYN

my mom's name is anderson . . .

ADAM

oh. are you twenty-five?

EVELYN

twenty-two. just . . . i skipped third grade.

ADAM

okay . . . (*beat.*) and the scars are . . .

EVELYN

i made it all up.

ADAM

got it. i got it . . . gemini at least?

EVELYN

no, pisces. sorry.

ADAM

don't be. hey, it's . . . *art.*

a moment of silence. they look at each other for a bit.

EVELYN

(*checking watch*) i should probably get going, i gotta
hook up with some guys from my department . . .

ADAM

alright.

EVELYN

. . . and i think the dean wants 'a word' with me, too.
(*ricky ricardo voice*) 'i got some 'splaining to do.'

ADAM

what's that from?

EVELYN

nothing. *i love lucy.*

ADAM

ahh, tv. that other great art form . . .

EVELYN

uh-huh. you coming?

ADAM

nah, not yet . . . (*holds up hands.*) don't worry, i'm not
gonna do anything to your stuff. no spray paint. i just . . .

EVELYN

i understand. go ahead.

ADAM

thanks . . .

EVELYN

the door locks if you just close it.

ADAM

great.

*evelyn smiles at him once more, but says nothing.
what's to say? she heads for the door but stops.*

EVELYN

. . . that one time.

ADAM

huh?

EVELYN

in your bed, one night, when you leaned over and
whispered in my ear . . . remember?

ADAM

'course. i remember everything about us.

EVELYN

and i whispered back to you, i said . . .

ADAM

i remember.

EVELYN

i meant that. i did.

ADAM

yeah?

EVELYN

yes.

ADAM

. . . oh.

*she starts to say something else but catches herself. she
goes out. adam stands alone in the quiet room,
looking about. he takes a few more cookies, eating
them as he wanders around and picks up items from*

his recent life with evelyn. he finally stops near the tv/vcr. suddenly, he pops in a tape and settles back on the floor. he finds the moment he is looking for . . . the exchange of whispers.

he presses 'play' and watches it. he rewinds and does it again. and again. he scoots over and pulls on his old jacket, huddling there on the ground. he watches the picture intently, but what is being said remains elusive. unheard. he continues.

silence. darkness.